A Teaspoon
of Poetry

Mariah Haney

ISBN 978-1-7331354-0-5

Foreword

My name is Mariah Haney. At the time of writing this I am 19 and will be turning 20 in a couple of days. When I was younger I discovered how much I enjoyed poetry while reading Shel Silverstein's <u>Where the Sidewalk Ends</u>. Over the course of several years I have been writing and compiling my own poetry, starting with *Being Different* when I was 11. Some of my poems are titled, many of them are not. I apologize for that, but trying to title them simply felt like attempting to fit a square peg in a round hole: awkward, unwieldy and out of place. I find poetry an enjoyable medium both to write and to read. It has been a lot of fun to write this book and I hope you enjoy it too.

Table of Contents

Writing

I'm writing a poem
Unlike anything I've written before
Because
It's alive
I feel its ebb
And its flow
Its breath
Sends shivers down my spine
Chills inexplicable
As I cradle in my heart
This thing called art

I Think in Ink

I think in ink
In lines and rhymes
The little eddied swirls of words
That soak into the page
It oozes
Raw and open
In little rivulets from heart and mind alike
And sometimes a torrent
That spirals down down
Down
And out through fervent fingers
In the click of keys
Or the scritch scratch of pen on paper
And bares open to the world
In ink
Myself

I Write

I write
With the hands of a young woman
Confident
And swift of stroke
In cursive and in print
The ebb and flow of script

But
I once wrote
With the fumbling hands of a child
Whose blocky letters
Crawled, uneven, across the page
As I began to learn the language –
Of the written word

And
Perhaps in the future I will write
With the shaking hands of an old woman
Pondering and deliberate
With a lifetime's worth of words behind
And who smiles at the ink stains
Pooled in the creases of her weathered skin

Lost

I got lost
Somewhere
Along the way
Between dreams
And reality
Today
A breath of air
A sigh
Of moments lapse
Amidst
Winding claustrophobia
Of ethereal
Perhaps

Stone

Nothing here is set in stone
It's all written in the sand
Todays, tomorrows, yesterdays
Blown away in the wind
It's going to get worse before it gets better
This storm that is life
Hold tight, hold fast
So that with laughter on our lips
We may set our weary hearts aside
And smile

A Pondering

A pondering,
Wandering,
Lackadaisical day
Just sittin' in the sun
Jumpin' puddles
Oh what fun
Books and board games
Playin' tag
Don't forget
Your pirate flag
Sun's a' settin'
In the west
S'mores and bonfires
Singin' loud
Stars are shinin'
Bright tonight
And, OH
What a day
To dance the night away
And dream again

Being Different

The door closes
As I walk to the bleachers
I sit down
Alone
No one waves
To me
No one calls
My name
Around me people talk
But I am silent
I sit
A book in my lap
Waiting for the bell to ring
All too soon it does
I stand, close my book
And walk out of the gym with the tidal wave of other children
Again the door closes
To them I am different
But to me I am normal

Now

Today, tomorrow, yesterday
One stays
The others dance
At its edges
Present, future, past
One stays
The others dance
At its edges
Four dancers
Two with memories
Two with possibilities
Two workers
Always here
And with now comes many uncertainties

One

We are all one in
A million and lost in
A sea of faces

Forwards and Backwards

Simply	Are
Simply be	You are
Simply be who	Who you are
Simply be who you	Be who you are
Simply be who you are	Simply be who you are
Live	Wonderful
Live, life	Is wonderful
Live, life is	Life is wonderful
Live, life is wonderful	Live, Life is wonderful
Make	Reality
Make dreams	Into reality
Make dreams into	Dreams into reality
Make dreams into reality	Make dreams into reality
Hate	Apart
Hate drives	World Apart
Hate drives the	The world apart
Hate drives the world	Drives the world apart
Hate drives the world apart	Hate drives the world apart
Love	Together
Love sews	Back together
Love sews it	It back together
Love sews it back	Sews it back together
Love sews it back together	Love sews it back together

Where do I Begin

Where do I begin
With all the weight of the stars
Underneath my skin

Gravity beyond
I dare not deign breathe again
As frost crests the sky

Heartbeat long and loud
Ocean roar beneath the crowd
Scorching tongue and raze

I Just Want

I just want to run
To fly
Feel the wind in my wings
Catch my breath
Take a step
On my journey of me

Spring

In the spring
When the breeze
Dances through the trees
A spin
On a whim
A song on the wind
Of the soft sound of chimes
And butterfly's wings

Butterfly

Whispers in the wind
And voices in the night
Take flight
There was something strange
About the way he stood there
Just so
Where even the grass –
Refused to grow
He spoke in a voice
Like stone
And told a tale
To no one
But I heard
A story told
But the words have faded
Long ago
And I wonder why
But still I cry
O'er the soft, soft wings of the butterfly
Wisdom's thoughts are nigh
Privy but to the child's eye
And I wonder why
But still I cry
O'er the soft, soft wings of the butterfly
All things of the earth

We have no different birth
And I wonder why
But still I cry
O'er the soft, soft wings of the butterfly
The child's heart knows
What words nor thoughts can express
And I wonder why
But still I cry
O'er the soft, soft wings of the butterfly
A story told
And the faded words
Have been inked in again
And I know why
But still I cry
O'er the soft, soft wings of the butterfly

The Griffolips

Beak of the bird
Roar of the lion
The Griffolips –
Soars through the sky
To land lightly on the cliffs
Golden, black or other colors
Gazing across the sky
Watching, waiting
For the right time to take flight
To soar freely through the skies
Then one by one
As the sun comes over the horizon
They spread their feathered wings
And take to the skies once more

Dragons

Swiftly running
Quickly flying
From above the tallest mountain
To the bottom of the oceans
This is where they roam
From the North
To the South
This is where they roam
Creatures of fire, ice
And many other things
Nonexistent in reality
But real to the imagination
Of whoever chooses to imagine them
Large or small
They are dragons

Lightning Flashes

Lightning flashes
And thunder crashes
A shadow outlined in the dark
A flash golden eyes
The glimmer of water on scales
And then it's gone
Until once again
Lightning flashes
And thunder crashes
A shadow outlined in the dark
Golden eyes gazing across the horizon
Toward the far off sea
And then it's gone
Until once again
Lightning flashes
And thunder crashes
A shadow outlined in the dark
Running across the fields
Toward the far off sea
Out of sight the dragon runs
And once again it's gone
Until far away
Lightning flashes
And thunder crashes
A shadow outlined in the dark

Freedom

Over land
Over sea
I fly freely
Through wind
Through spray
I fly freely
Adrenalin keeps me going
Pumping through my body
To the beat of my wings and heart
A strong steady slow beat
And as the beat shuts out the world
I fly freely

Storms roll in
But I do not falter
As the water drums against my scales
And soon thunder crashes
And lightning flashes
As fire flares in the sky
And still I fly freely

Tiger

The hiding tiger
Shivers, whiskers aquiver,
Then leaps to the sky

Dark

Snake in the dark sea
A stream of dark in darkness
A black ribbon seen

Birdsong

Singing birds are here
Floating in a pale blue sky
Sing to the morning

Inferno

A high plume of smoke
All fire raging, eyes blazing
With no thought of end

Wolf

The wolf's howling song
Rising to the moon, fragile
Shattered by morning

Dragons in the Firelight

AROO!, AROOOO!
Sing the dragons
As they twist and turn and dive and twirl in the sky
AROO!, AROOOO!
Sing the dragons
As the flickering firelight casts their shadows all over
Soaring through the skies
They are wild and free
AROO!, AROOOO!
Sing the dragons
Long after the fire has turned to ember
And from ember to ash
Still they sing on
On and on and on it goes
Even while the dawn is breaking
We are wild!
We are free!
They sing
And yet once the sun is over the horizon
Not a dragon to be seen
There is no trace of them
Not a scale or feather nor tuft of fur
Nothing to suggest that they were ever there
Nothing that is except for the ashes of a fire

Alight

Fire, fire burning bright
What dost thou see in the night
Stoke my heart's desire

One Dimensional Tree

A one dimensional tree,
Is not very much you see ~
For one dimension is not even two ~
And that much less than three

The Drawing

Pencils fly across the paper
Bit by bit
The picture comes together
Hearts
For Valentine's Day
Eggs
For Easter
Cats, bats, ghosts, and jack-o-lanterns
For Halloween
Turkeys
For Thanksgiving
Trees, ornaments, lights, presents, and Bible scenes
For Christmas
All together to make
A drawing

Journey

A boy set about on a journey
Happy as could be
He let the world pass by him
And all the while people came and went
Some to lead and guide by wisdom
Some to befuddle and confuse with lies and trickery
There were with him on the day
When the track went on and split
His friends alone and no one else
They stood and looked at the paths before them
One worn and smooth far as the eye could see
The other covered in vines and thorns
Then one by one they left him
Standing there alone
And all went down the easy path
Yet still he stood
Unable to decide
How long had he stood there?
He did not know
When there came someone who asked him
"Which way are you to go?"
He simply shrugged and shook his head
None had spoken to him as long as he had stood there
Then she began to talk
And showed him such wonder

They asked each other of their journeys
Then hand in hand they went
Down the path with vines and thorns
Where they helped each other all the way
And at the end was the most amazing thing
That they had ever seen

A Teaspoon of Poetry

A teaspoon of poetry
A measure of thought
All good things
But all for naught
Without a cup of courage
Wait, anticipate
Dreams alive and breathing
Worry, hurry
Watch them wilt
Without a cup of courage
Talent, skill and merits
Curbed, stunted, pinned
Pine and whine, despair
Without a cup of courage
For others to cultivate
Find your courage hold it high
Behold the dragon's grin
O' eyes to see
O' heart to beat
Lord give me strength!
Just a cup of courage
Stand tall
Stand strong
Find your cup of courage
Take the leap

Bridge the gap
Stand firm on the other side
Follow your dreams!
Spread your wings!
All it takes
Is a cup of courage

www.ingramcontent.com/pod-product-compliance
Lightning Source LLC
Chambersburg PA
CBHW031336040426
42443CB00005B/366